Media Literacy (BrightPoint Press) (Library Binding)

8/18/2021

Titles in set: 5

Total for set: $159.75

Hi-Lo YA nonfiction. Media Literacy explores how people get their news and whether they can trust it. Readers will learn key media

---

Distinguishing Fact from Opinion $31.95

Opinions can sometimes be disguised as facts, and readers looking only at opinion pieces may develop an incomplete picture of the news topic being discussed. Distinguishing Fact from Opinion examines t...

#2245458 M. Ventura   Available:08/01/2021   80 pgs

Grade:678   Dewey:302.23   LEX:770

How Social Media Impacts News $31.95

Social media allows people to stay connected and share news quickly. How Social Media Impacts News examines the benefits of spreading news fast, but it also highlights the dangers of incomplete or fake...

#2245459 T. Gagne   Available:08/01/2021   80 pgs

Grade:678   Dewey:302   LEX:770

Identifying Fake News $31.95

Sometimes information that is posted online, printed in papers, and talked about on television isn't true. Identifying Fake News examines why fake information spreads, the dangers it can cause, and how...

#2245463 R. Van   Available:08/01/2021   80 pgs

Grade:678   Dewey:302   LEX:760

Identifying Media Bias $31.95

Everyone has their own opinions, but journalists are supposed to keep theirs out of stories. Their job is to report the news and not push people into thinking a certain way. When stories are slanted to...

#2245464 T. Gagne   Available:08/01/2021   80 pgs

Grade:678   Dewey:302.23

Legitimate News Sources $31.95

Not every news article has a responsible journalist writing it, and some even try to push readers into thinking a certain way. Legitimate News Sources gives readers tips on how to navigate the seemingl...

#2245465 A. Buckey   Available:08/01/2021   80 pgs

Grade:678   Dewey:302   LEX:780

MEDIA LITERACY

DISTINGUISHING FACT FROM OPINION

by Marne Ventura

BrightPoint Press

San Diego, CA

BrightPoint Press

© 2022 BrightPoint Press
an imprint of ReferencePoint Press, Inc.
Printed in the United States

For more information, contact:
BrightPoint Press
PO Box 27779
San Diego, CA 92198
www.BrightPointPress.com

LIBRARY OF CONGRESS CATALOGING-IN-PUBLICATION DATA

Names: Ventura, Marne, author.
Title: Distinguishing fact from opinion / Marne Ventura.
Description: San Diego, CA : BrightPoint Press, 2022. | Series: Media literacy | Includes
    bibliographical references and index. | Audience: Grades 7-9
Identifiers: LCCN 2021012602 (print) | LCCN 2021012603 (eBook) | ISBN 9781678201944
    (hardcover) | ISBN 9781678201951 (eBook)
Subjects: LCSH: Media literacy--Juvenile literature.
Classification: LCC P96.M4 V46 2022 (print) | LCC P96.M4 (eBook) | DDC 302.23--dc23
LC record available at https://lccn.loc.gov/2021012602
LC eBook record available at https://lccn.loc.gov/2021012603

CONTENTS

AT A GLANCE

- A fact is information that can be proven true. An opinion is a person's view or judgment.

- To figure out whether something is true, people can look at primary sources. Some people might use the scientific method to test a hypothesis. Others might rely on empirical data. These things help people establish whether something is a fact.

- Opinions can't be proven. But everyone has opinions. They're often formed by people's views of the facts.

- Starting in the late 1900s, some TV news networks began to broadcast content all day. In addition to fact-based reporting, they also had shows featuring people's opinions.

- In news stories, good reporters explain where their facts came from. They also clearly quote people's opinions.

- Sometimes people take opinions to be facts. This can have real-world consequences. For instance, during the COVID-19 pandemic, some people believed politicians' opinions over scientific facts. This led to health consequences for some of those people.

- A reporter's bias can sneak into news. Sometimes the person's bias is clear. Other times it's less obvious. A reporter's bias can influence readers' opinions. News consumers need to think critically about the sources they find.

SEARCHING FOR FACTS AND OPINIONS

Mark powered up his computer. He was ready to do research for a school report. His assignment was to find two facts and two opinions about **climate change**. He typed "climate change" into a search engine. Millions of results popped up.

Good school research starts with finding legitimate sources.

Mark read through a number of different articles. He was trying to find a good, legitimate source. He clicked on a *Scientific American* article. It listed a lot of information about climate change. Mark had heard of the website before, but he wasn't exactly sure how credible it was. He went to the site's "About" page. He read that the publication was created in 1845. Its mission was to write about new discoveries and research. The article's author had a lot of experience writing about science topics. The article also had a date, showing it was published recently. Mark knew these were signs that he could trust the information on the site.

Mark wrote down two facts he found in the article about climate change. First,

People have protested the use of fossil fuels.

he learned that humans use a lot of **fossil fuels**, such as oil and coal. These release carbon dioxide into the atmosphere. Carbon dioxide contributes to climate change. Second, Mark learned that Earth is warming and glaciers are melting. He was able to double-check that these facts were true. The author listed his sources. Mark went to those websites and read the same information. The websites listed were from legitimate sources, such as NASA.

Next, Mark found a couple of opinions about climate change. The opinions talked about energy sources that are not bad for the environment. One expert said that people should switch from fossil fuels to wind and solar power. A second expert said people should use more nuclear power instead. Mark knew that these opinions were based on people's interpretations of

Some people believe more wind turbines should be built to reduce fossil fuel use.

the facts. There was no way for Mark to prove that these opinions were the best courses of action.

NEWS, FACTS, AND OPINIONS

Today, people get information from a variety of news sources. These can be from print, broadcast, and internet sources. Many news organizations put out information that is accurate. Their statements are based solely on facts. Sometimes news includes opinions. But good reporters make sure opinions are labeled clearly. That way, they're not confused with facts.

However, some news sources may not check their information to make sure it's true. Opinions may slip into news stories and be presented as facts. Some sources may even present opinions as facts on purpose. Being able to tell the difference between fact and opinion is an important

Newspapers often have clearly labeled opinion sections.

skill. With so much information available in today's world, readers or listeners who are critical thinkers can find the facts they need to form their own opinions. Having opinions rooted in facts can help people make good decisions.

CHAPTER ONE

WHAT ARE FACTS AND OPINIONS?

A fact is something that can be proven true. For instance, it's a fact that NASA landed a **rover** on Mars in 2021. People can verify this by checking NASA's website. They can see pictures the rover took on Mars. They can watch the landing video. They can even hear audio taken from the planet's surface.

*In 2021, the Mars rover **Perseverance** took high-resolution photos of the planet's surface.*

An opinion is a judgment or view about a situation. "It was a waste of money to send a rover to Mars" is an opinion. "Getting a rover to Mars is the most amazing thing humans have ever done" is also an opinion.

People often discuss their opinions with others.

It's important for people to know how

to distinguish between facts and opinions.

That way, people can better understand the

information they read or hear. Knowing the

difference between facts and opinions helps

people make informed decisions in their

everyday lives. People can prove something

is a fact by using empirical data, reliable

sources, and the scientific method. People cannot prove that opinions are true. But they can evaluate them and see whether they're supported by facts. Daniel Patrick Moynihan was a US senator from New York. He once said, "Everyone is entitled to his own opinion, but not to his own facts."[1]

USING DATA AND SOURCES

People sometimes use empirical data to figure out whether information is true or false. Empirical data is information people get through observation. They see, hear, feel, smell, or taste the world around them. Football fans know the final score of the

Microscopes allow scientists to study and get data from things they would not otherwise be able to see.

game because they watched the event. The

chef knows the milk is spoiled because it

smells sour.

However, people can't always be present

to observe whether information is true or

false. For example, people who want to know more about history can't go back in time. They must rely on other sources of information, such as primary sources.

Primary sources are firsthand accounts of something. They can also be direct evidence of a situation or event. Imagine someone wants to learn more about Abraham Lincoln. She can't talk to the late president. To learn more about him, she needs to do research. One way to do this is to visit the Library of Congress website. It is run by the US government. It posts speeches and letters that were written by

Lincoln. These are primary sources. The information is reliable. The words in the documents come directly from the former president. Secondary sources can also be useful. These sources interpret or analyze a situation or event. Authors of reliable secondary sources often use primary sources to write their text. A book or an encyclopedia article about Lincoln is a secondary source.

THE SCIENTIFIC METHOD

Reliable facts also come from experts. For instance, to learn about space a person might get information from NASA scientists.

Museums often have primary sources on display, such as letters, newspapers, and photos.

These experts gather factual information and write reports. They do this by using the scientific method.

The scientific method is a system. It is used to find answers to scientific questions. Researchers use certain steps to study and learn things. First, they define a question. Next, they form a guess. This is also known as a hypothesis. Scientists then test the

FACTS CAN CHANGE

Facts can change over time. One example is the minimum hourly wage set by the US government. This rate is the least amount that employers can pay their workers. In 1956, the federal minimum wage was $1.00. In early 2021, it was $7.25. Scientific facts can change too. This knowledge evolves as researchers gather more evidence. They may draw updated conclusions based on new evidence.

hypothesis. They do this by conducting experiments. They analyze the data. Then they interpret the results.

Scientists report whether the results support the hypothesis. Other scientists repeat the experiments to test the results over time. When many scientists get the same results over a long period of time, they agree that there is good evidence to support or reject the hypothesis.

Neil deGrasse Tyson is an American astrophysicist. He notes, "The good thing about science is that it's true whether or not you believe in it."[2]

DEBATING OPINIONS

Opinions are subjective. That means they're influenced by people's viewpoints or feelings. For this reason, people cannot prove opinions with empirical data or the scientific method. Instead, people debate their opinions. In order to make their cases,

IT'S A THEORY

People sometimes respond to arguments by saying, "That's only a theory." They usually mean that the statement is a guess that lacks evidence. But for scientists, the term *theory* has a different meaning. In science, a theory is a well-supported explanation of something in the natural world. Gravity and evolution are both examples of well-tested scientific theories.

they use facts to support their views. Better evidence may make their opinions more persuasive.

For example, scientists around the world have gathered evidence about climate change. They know Earth is warming. They've discovered that Earth's average temperature has increased over the past 150 years. The evidence shows human activities have caused climate change. Scientists are concerned that climate change is harmful to life on Earth.

Science proves that climate change is real. But people have different opinions

TELLING FACTS FROM OPINIONS

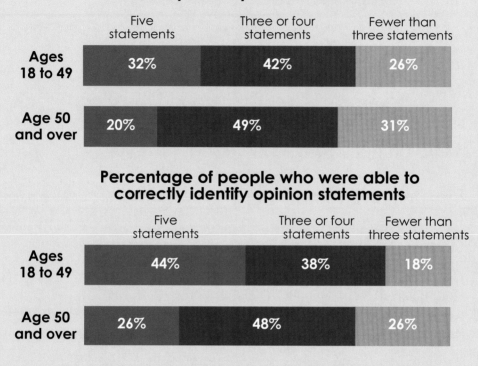

Percentage of people who were able to correctly identify factual statements

	Five statements	Three or four statements	Fewer than three statements
Ages 18 to 49	32%	42%	26%
Age 50 and over	20%	49%	31%

Percentage of people who were able to correctly identify opinion statements

	Five statements	Three or four statements	Fewer than three statements
Ages 18 to 49	44%	38%	18%
Age 50 and over	26%	48%	26%

Source: Jeffery Gottfried and Elizabeth Grieco, "Younger Americans Are Better Than Older Americans at Telling Factual News Statements from Opinions," Pew Research Center, October 23, 2018. www.pewresearch.org.

In 2018, the Pew Research Center did a survey. It gave participants five opinion statements and five factual statements. People had to distinguish between them. It found that people ages eighteen to forty-nine were better at determining facts from opinions compared with older adults.

about what needs to be done about
it. Some people think the government
should create laws. They want the laws
to encourage people to use **renewable
energy** instead of fossil fuels. Renewable
energy, such as solar and wind power, is
better for the environment. Others believe
the government should not interfere. They
think changing energy sources might cause
job losses. Both of these are opinions.
They're formed from people's evaluations of
the facts.

CHAPTER TWO

WHAT IS THE HISTORY OF FACTS AND OPINIONS IN THE MEDIA?

People have been sharing news for centuries. Before modern media, messengers carried news from one place to another. In 1000 CE and likely earlier, town criers spread news. They called

Some people today put on performances as town criers.

out information in the streets. The news

included new laws and royal proclamations.

People who heard the news passed it on by

word of mouth.

Being able to print and distribute materials let people share news easily.

THE FIRST AMERICAN NEWSPAPERS

Johannes Gutenberg invented the printing press in the mid-1400s. The machine allowed people to make a large number of printed materials cheaply. By using the printing press, people were able to spread knowledge across Europe and eventually

beyond. However, it wasn't until the 1600s

that newspapers really started to take off.

In 1690, Benjamin Harris published

a newspaper in Boston. It was the first

LIBEL CASE

In 1735, John Peter Zenger was arrested. He was put on trial. Zenger had been publishing the *New York Weekly Journal*. The journal had printed criticisms about the British colonial governor. Some articles said the governor rigged elections and committed other crimes. For publishing these articles, Zenger was accused of libel. Libel is a false printed statement. It damages a person's reputation. In the end, the jury found Zenger not guilty. That's because the statements he published were true.

newspaper in England's North American colonies. The paper featured opinions about the unfairness of English rule.

Printed news became more common in the years that followed. Samuel Morse invented the telegraph in 1844. A telegraph works by sending electrical signals through wires. This allowed reporters to send information from one location to another quickly. In 1866, a telegraph line was laid across the Atlantic Ocean. Now, news could be exchanged quickly between the United States and Europe. By the end of the

For many years, newspapers were the main way people got their news.

1800s, newspapers were being published in many cities across the United States.

This new industry created jobs. It brought in money for publishers. Journalists and salespeople were also involved in the industry. Some papers reported important news to the public. The publishers checked to make sure their facts were accurate. They labeled opinions. But some publishers found that they could sell more papers using different tactics. They had entertaining, exciting, or shocking headlines. They printed false statements. They didn't label opinions. These papers made up information or exaggerated facts. They did this to make stories more interesting.

Over time, readers realized they were not seeing fact-based reporting. They began to distrust newspapers. In response, some news organizations, such as the *New York Times*, began setting standards for truthful reporting. In addition, universities began to offer programs in journalism. They taught students how to do fair and honest reporting. Also, in 1909 the

THE FIVE Ws AND AN H

Journalism students learn to include *who*, *what*, *when*, *where*, *why*, and *how* in the first paragraph of a news story. This practice ensures that readers get the basic facts quickly. In the early days of news, reporters used telegraphs to send stories. The lines often went down. They learned to send the most important facts first. Another reason for the style was that start-up newspapers didn't have a lot money. Paper, ink, printing presses, and reporters cost money. Shorter stories were cheaper to make.

Society of Professional Journalists (SPJ) was founded. The SPJ works to make sure journalists report accurate, fair, and complete information.

RADIO AND TV NEWS

In the 1920s, NBC and CBS began reporting news over the radio. Politicians gave speeches or made announcements through this form of media too. About 83 percent of US households listened to radio news by 1940.

In the 1940s, NBC and CBS also began broadcasting news on television. During these shows, a person off-screen read

It takes teams of people to put news programs together.

the news while a prerecorded video of the topic was shown. These first shows were on the air once a week for ten minutes. By 1949, ABC had a nightly news program as well. Certain TV news anchors, such as Walter Cronkite, became well-known. They were trusted by the American public. In the 1960s, advances in technology meant

Today, journalists often report live from news scenes.

that news could be shown live. Another

breakthrough was the ability to show film in

color. News programs were broadcast daily

for thirty minutes.

In 1980, CNN began to broadcast

news all day, every day. CNN was known

for being the first to report on live events around the world. In addition to the constant live news, CNN had weekly shows. Hosts interviewed guests to get their take on the news. As time went by, other channels such as Fox News and MSNBC began to offer these programs too. Both of these channels started running in 1996. They had factual news. But they also had guest experts. These experts gave their opinions about politics, culture, and other topics. In addition, some shows from these stations are based entirely on the opinions of the hosts and their guests.

THE INTERNET AND SOCIAL MEDIA

During the 1990s, news publishers launched websites. Now, people could see news online. They could read both factual and opinion-based stories from a variety of sources.

Social media platforms started to take off in the early 2000s. People began posting photos, information, and opinions on social media. They also started sharing links to news stories. The Pew Research Center did a poll in 2020. It found that 53 percent of US adults got their news from social media platforms.

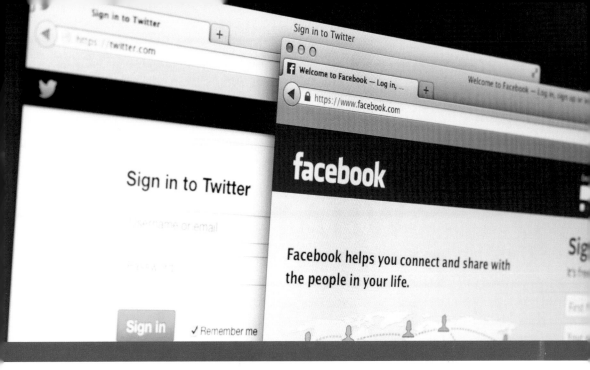

Social media platforms, such as Twitter and Facebook, remain popular today.

This trend can make distinguishing between facts and opinions hard. Anyone can post information on social media. The content in the post may not be true. The post could have opinions disguised as facts. It is up to the reader or listener to think critically about the content.

CHAPTER THREE

WHAT ARE EXAMPLES OF FACTS AND OPINIONS?

Today, news is everywhere. People can read about any subject at any time of the day. Some sources of information are honest and fair. Other sources have inaccurate information. They may present opinions as facts. Knowing the difference

People can easily access news stories on smart devices.

between facts and opinions can influence

how people react to situations.

THE COVID-19 PANDEMIC

In December 2019, the first case of COVID-19 was reported in Wuhan, China. COVID-19 is a disease. It's caused by a virus. The virus spread quickly around the world, causing a **pandemic**. Millions of people died.

At first, scientists didn't fully understand the virus. They made recommendations based on the facts they had. At the start of the pandemic, the US Centers for Disease Control and Prevention (CDC) said most healthy people didn't need to wear face masks. But as time went on, experts

When COVID-19 started spreading across the United States, many people wanted to stay up to date on the news.

learned more about how the virus spread.

They realized masks were helpful. The CDC

gave new advice based on new facts. It said that everyone should wear masks.

However, people spread their own opinions about face coverings. President Donald Trump gave many opinions on the subject. In August 2020, he said, "Maybe [masks are] great, and maybe they're just good. Maybe they're not so good."[3] Trump's statements were sometimes at odds with the scientific facts, which said masks were helpful. Some people around the country shared similar opinions. For instance, a woman named Susan Wiles didn't wear a mask in public spaces. People got upset with her. But she didn't believe the facts that scientists presented. She said, "I don't fall for this. It's not what they say it is."[4] By April 2021, more than 550,000 Americans had died from COVID-19.

TO MASK OR NOT TO MASK

During the COVID-19 pandemic, many US state governors said people had to wear masks in public. They were following the CDC's advice. But a small number of people still didn't want to wear masks. The Pew Research Center did a survey in 2020. It found that 65 percent of US adults typically wore masks in public. About 15 percent of adults said they wore masks sometimes. Only 9 percent of people said they hardly ever did this. Just 7 percent of people said they never wore masks. The rest said they didn't go to public spaces at all.

WORDS, ACTIONS, AND CONSEQUENCES

Believing people's opinions on COVID-19 over scientific facts may have had real-world consequences. Robert Hahn used to work for the CDC as an epidemiologist. This is the study of disease control. Hahn wanted to know how many people might have died by listening to opinions over facts. In particular, he looked at Trump's comments about mask wearing. Hahn examined data. He estimated that up to 12,000 people may have died by believing Trump's negative opinions on masks.

Some people protested when asked to wear masks.

Others were also interested in the consequences of not wearing masks. There is scientific evidence that wearing masks helped prevent COVID-19 from spreading. However, not all states made people wear them throughout the pandemic. A study was published in early 2021. Researchers from the Massachusetts Institute of Technology and the University of British Columbia did the study. They looked at data from the pandemic. The data was from the start of the pandemic to the end of May 2020. They found that if all workers who interacted with the public had been required

Some grocery stores had to close after areas in Texas lost power. Those that stayed open had long lines of people waiting to get inside.

to wear masks, between 19,000 and 47,000

US lives might have been saved.

TEXAS POWER OUTAGE

In February 2021, a winter storm hit Texas.

The area had record-low temperatures.

Snow and ice coated many roads.

The state's electrical grid couldn't keep up

with the demand for energy. Many people

lost power. At one point, 4 million houses were affected. People were cold, and some froze to death. Many people were unable to get food, safe water, medical help, or other necessities.

Texas's power grid is run by the Electric Reliability Council of Texas. This agency said the power outage may have been caused in part by frozen wind turbines. Wind turbines are a form of renewable energy. The agency also said that limited fossil fuel supplies were to blame too. But some people who didn't like renewable energy used the situation as an opportunity

Wind turbines in colder climates often have features to keep them working in the winter. Most of Texas's turbines didn't have these features.

to spread their opinions. They wanted to put all the blame on renewable energy.

For example, Greg Abbott is the governor of Texas. He said that using renewable energy sources "thrust Texas into a situation where it was lacking power on a statewide basis."[5] Other politicians jumped on this narrative too. Dan Crenshaw is a Texas representative. He said, "This is what happens when you force the grid to rely in part on wind as a power source. When weather conditions get bad as they did this week . . . renewable energy like wind isn't there when you need it."[6]

However, experts said renewable energy sources were not responsible for most of the state's power outage. Most were due to fossil fuels. However, that didn't stop people's opinions about renewable energy from spreading. Sometimes people state their opinions as facts. When people hear politicians do this, they may think the politicians have more information than most people. They may quickly believe what the politicians say. To avoid this, people can develop good critical thinking skills. This can help them figure out which news is fact-based and which is opinion.

SPREADING OPINIONS

Many people had opinions about the Texas power outage. They posted their thoughts online. Well-known people did this too. But some of them presented their opinions as facts. For example, Fox News has many well-known hosts for its shows. These hosts have a lot of followers. Some of them said wind turbines were to blame for the blackouts in Texas. Their posts had more than 15.8 million views on Facebook.

CHAPTER FOUR

HOW CAN I DISTINGUISH BETWEEN FACTS AND OPINIONS?

People get information from a wide variety of sources. They read newspapers and magazines. They listen to radio and television broadcasts. They download podcasts. They visit websites, blogs, and social media. People are

People don't need televisions to listen to news reports. They can often find clips online.

constantly reporting news as it happens.

With so much information available, people

need to figure out which statements are

true. They can also work to figure out which

opinions are based on facts.

Journalists often interview experts while putting together news stories.

LOOK FOR THE SOURCE

People often read or hear statements

that are presented as facts. They can ask

themselves certain questions to figure out if

the statements are true. One question they

can ask is, does the statement tell where

the information came from? **Reputable** journalists say where they got their facts. They cite reports or experts. People can do some independent research too. They can search out the reports or experts noted. They can see if the information matches up.

People can do this with any type of news source. For example, many people on social media aren't experts on the topics they post about. But they may share information anyway. People can double-check statements they see on social media. For example, if someone saw a Facebook post that said, "We might have a blizzard this week," the person could go to the National Weather Service website. He or she could also see if the local news station had any information on this. The person could check whether the statement is true.

Opinions are easy to identify if they are labeled. Journalists often put people's opinions in quotes. Sometimes they paraphrase what the person said. When this happens, the journalists still need to make it clear that it is someone's opinion.

Sometimes opinions aren't as easy to recognize. They may sound like facts. But certain words may signal that a

Legitimate news sources often have obvious tabs on their websites telling people which information is fact-based and which is opinion.

statement is an opinion rather than a fact.

Judgment words may be used. These

words can include *good*, *bad*, *better*, *worse*,

worthwhile, and *worthless*. Absolute words

such as *nobody, everybody, never,* or *always* are also signal words for opinions. For example, "The new gymnasium at the high school will cost taxpayers $24,000," is a fact that can be checked. On the other hand, "Building a new gymnasium at the high school is a good use of taxpayer money," is an opinion.

People can research opinions. An opinion such as, "My town has the best weather in the world," can't be proven. But someone could look up the weather records for the area. If the person enjoys warm temperatures and the weather in the

People may not always agree, but they can discuss their different opinions respectfully.

town averaged 70°F (21°C), he or she might

agree with the opinion.

WATCH OUT FOR BIAS

There are other questions people can ask

themselves when distinguishing between

facts and opinions. They can ask whether

the source of the information has a **bias**. When authors, reporters, or speakers have biases, they tend to see things in a certain way. This can slip into how they present information. They may let their biases overshadow facts. Or they may believe that their biased opinions are actually facts.

For example, a weather reporter without a bias on the topic might report, "The weather today is 70°F (21°C)." Someone with a bias in favor of cool weather might say, "The weather today is too warm." Another person with a bias in favor of hot weather might say, "The weather today is

Responsible journalists do their best to keep their biases out of stories.

too cold." In this simple example, it's easy to

see that someone's opinion on the weather

is being shared.

Bias isn't always obvious. And it can be

harmful. Individuals may be biased against

certain groups of people. This can appear

in news reporting. For example, people

often protest things in society that they don't like. There have been many protests regarding police brutality toward people of color. Danielle Kilgo is a professor of journalism. She works at Indiana University. Kilgo knows that people's opinions can be shaped by what they see on the news. She said, "This gives journalists a lot of power when it comes to driving the narrative of a demonstration."[7] Kilgo looked at how the news treated different protests. She found that movements focusing on Black and Indigenous people's rights weren't as fairly reported on as other types of protests.

Stereotypes can lead to discriminatory behavior.

They were shown as more violent and threatening. This type of reporting can shape people's opinions. It can make them believe harmful **stereotypes** about people.

Audiences can't avoid seeing bias in the media, but they can identify it. They can ask which point of view the news is reporting. Are any viewpoints getting left out? They can also look carefully at the news report and see if it's playing off of stereotypes. For example, if a news outlet talks only about Black people when referencing crime, it may be biased against people of color.

SPOTTING STEREOTYPES

A stereotype is an oversimplified idea about a thing or person. People who believe stereotypes may think all members of a group have similar traits. Some of the most common stereotypes are based on gender, age, religion, race, and ethnicity. An example of a stereotype is, "Teenagers don't care about politics." Stereotypes are inaccurate. And they can be harmful. When reading the news, people should think critically about the information. They should pay attention to whether it uses stereotypes.

In addition, people can look at the language in a story. Are any loaded words being used? These words may show a reporter's bias. They can include terms such as *deserves*. Identifying biased opinions can stop people from adopting the same mindset. Instead, people can look up facts on their own. They can base their opinions on those.

Certain news sources have reputations for bias. For example, Fox News is known for being conservative. MSNBC is known for being liberal. One good way for readers to understand bias is to read stories on the same topic from different sources. How are the stories the same? How are they different? Does one story include facts that the other story leaves out? Do the stories include opinions? Are they labeled as opinions?

BE A CRITICAL THINKER

Some online news outlets and social media creators want to keep people on their sites for as long as possible. In order to do this, they find out things about the reader. For instance, many people look up information using search engines. A computer program notes which sites the reader chooses.

Looking critically at news outlets and the information presented can help people avoid unreliable sources.

Then the program posts more choices that are similar to the ones the reader picked. Because the information matches the reader's interests, the reader stays online longer. This may be good for the reader. It can help her quickly find sources that she wants. But the programs can also lead to one-sided information. Readers need to make sure the information they are being given is accurate and complete.

Critical thinking is the best defense in spotting facts and opinions. People can go through a checklist to see whether a source is reliable. For instance, reliable

FACT-CHECKING SITES

There are several websites that investigate news stories. They report on whether the information in the story is accurate. Examples of fact-checking sites are PolitiFact.com, FactCheck.org, and Snopes.com.

articles often list the author. They also state the author's qualifications. Good articles typically list the date the piece was published too. In addition, readers should think critically about the content they are reading. Some articles may be disguised as news stories. They may actually be promoting products or simply trying to push opinions onto readers.

Learning to distinguish between fact and opinion is important. When people are able to analyze their news, they can come to their own conclusions. They can make the best decisions for themselves.

GLOSSARY

bias

a prejudice that influences one's opinions and beliefs, sometimes unfairly

climate change

the human-caused change in Earth's weather and climate patterns

fossil fuels

fuel sources made up of animal and plant remains from millions of years ago

pandemic

an outbreak of a disease that spreads across the globe

renewable energy

energy from sources that can't be used up, such as solar and wind

reputable

to have a good standing and be trusted by many people

rover

a vehicle that explores the surface of another planet or moon

stereotypes

widely held but simplified ideas and images of people or things

SOURCE NOTES

CHAPTER ONE: WHAT ARE FACTS AND OPINIONS?

1. Quoted in "An American Original," *Vanity Fair*, October 2010. www.vanityfair.com.

2. Quoted in Neil deGrasse Tyson, "The Good Thing About Science Is That It's True Whether or Not You Believe in It," *Twitter*, June 14, 2013. https://twitter.com.

CHAPTER THREE: WHAT ARE EXAMPLES OF FACTS AND OPINIONS?

3. Quoted in Daniel Victor, Lew Serviss, and Azi Paybarah, "In His Own Words, Trump on the Coronavirus and Masks," *New York Times*, October 2, 2020. www.nytimes.com.

4. Quoted in Tara McKelvey, "Coronavirus: Why Are Americans So Angry About Masks?" *BBC*, July 20, 2020. www.bbc.com.

5. Quoted in Holmes Lybrand and Tara Subramaniam, "Fact-Checking the Texas Energy-Failure Blame Game," *CNN*, February 19, 2021. www.cnn.com.

6. Quoted in Lybrand and Subramaniam, "Fact-Checking the Texas Energy-Failure Blame Game."

CHAPTER FOUR: HOW CAN I DISTINGUISH BETWEEN FACTS AND OPINIONS?

7. Danielle Kilgo, "Riot or Resistance? The Way the Media Frames the Unrest in Minneapolis Will Shape the Public's View of Protest," *Nieman Lab*, May 30, 2020. www.niemanlab.org.

FOR FURTHER RESEARCH

BOOKS

Robin Terry Brown, *Breaking the News*. Washington, DC: National Geographic Kids, 2020.

Lisa A. McPartland, *The Importance of Good Sources*. New York: PowerKids Press, 2019.

R. L. Van, *Identifying Fake News*. San Diego, CA: BrightPoint Press, 2022.

INTERNET SOURCES

"'Fake News,' Lies and Propaganda: How to Sort Fact from Fiction," *University of Michigan Library*, January 12, 2021. https://guides.lib.umich.edu.

"How to Be an Expert Fact-Checker," *National Geographic Kids*, n.d. https://kids.nationalgeographic.com.

Kaiser Moffat, "The Importance of Media Literacy," *Young Leaders of the Americas Initiative*, n.d. https://ylai.state.gov.

WEBSITES

Crash Course: Navigating Digital Information
https://thecrashcourse.com/courses/navigatingdigitalinfo

The Crash Course website has a section that helps visitors evaluate online information.

Evaluating News
https://guides.csbsju.edu/c.php?g=621995&p=4332689

The College of Saint Benedict and Saint John's University give tips on how to identify fake news. The website offers information on the best ways to evaluate websites and images for accuracy.

PBS: Media Literacy Tips
https://pbslearningmedia.org/resource/media-literacy-tips/srl-curriculum

PBS has tips and videos that people can watch to increase their media literacy skills.

INDEX

IMAGE CREDITS

ABOUT THE AUTHOR

Marne Ventura is the author of more than one hundred books for children. A former elementary school teacher, she holds a master's degree in reading and language development from the University of California. Marne's nonfiction titles cover a wide range of topics, including STEM, arts and crafts, food and cooking, biographies, health, and survival. Her fiction series, the Worry Warriors, tells the story of four brave kids who learn to conquer their fears. Marne and her husband live on the central coast of California.